Getting Married
and Other Mistakes

BARBARA SLATE

OTHER PRESS
NEW YORK

Production Editor: Yvonne E. Cárdenas
Lettering and design: Danica Novgorodoff

10 9 8 7 6 5 4 3 2 1

Library of Congress Cataloging-in-Publication Data

Slate, Barbara.
  Getting married and other mistakes / by Barbara Slate.
      p. cm.
  ISBN 978-1-59051-535-8 (pbk. : acid-free paper) — ISBN 978-1-59051-536-5 (e book)
  1. Self-realization in women—Comic books, strips, etc. 2. Graphic novels. I. Title.
  PN6727.S544G48 2012
  741.5'973—dc23
                    2011049729

This book is dedicated to Richard Minsky and Richard C. Levy, both born January 7, 1947, my lucky day!

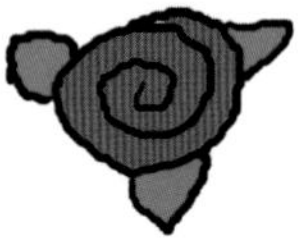

This is a picture of me on my wedding day.

I stare at the photograph and wonder... Who was that girl? What was she thinking? Was she in love?

I look happy...

or is that sadness in my eyes?

Did I know all along I was making a big mistake?

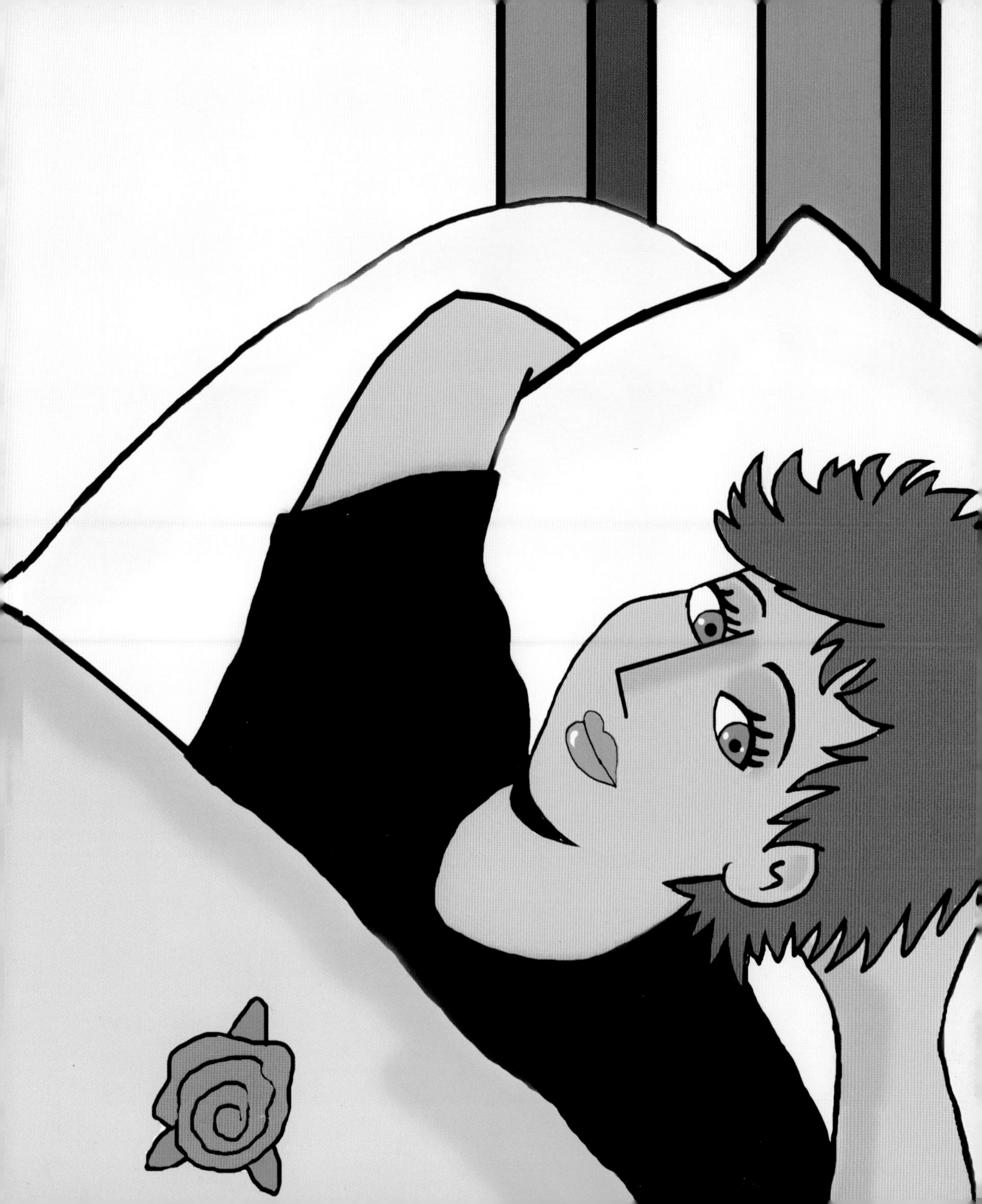

I was married for 7 years when...

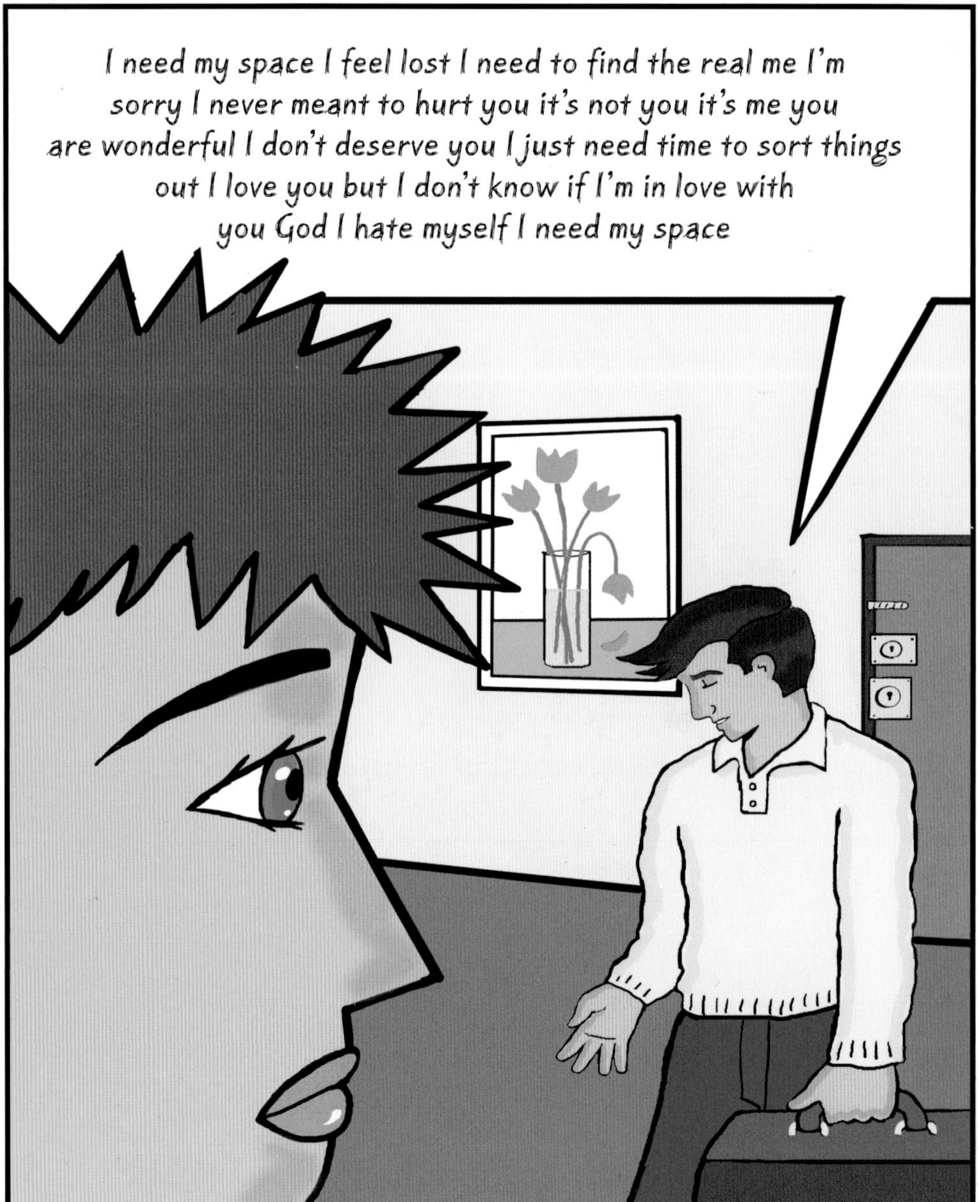

I believed John needed his space. *Who doesn't?* We lived in a box. A big box by *New York City* standards, but nonetheless a box.

I thought he'd go away for a day or two and then...

After all, we did take a vow to love each other "till death do us part." Silly me, I took my vows seriously.

It wasn't until the MESSAGE FROM HELL that I knew my marriage was in serious trouble...

My brain went on lockdown.

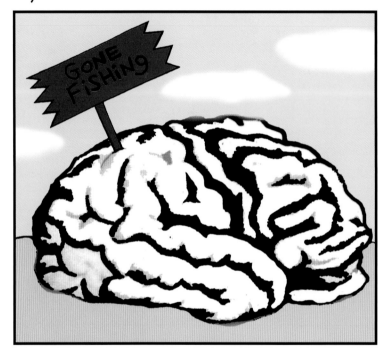

It had to—otherwise all the lies, deceits, and betrayals that flooded my mind would have made my head explode.

His lies were so unbelievable I had to believe him!

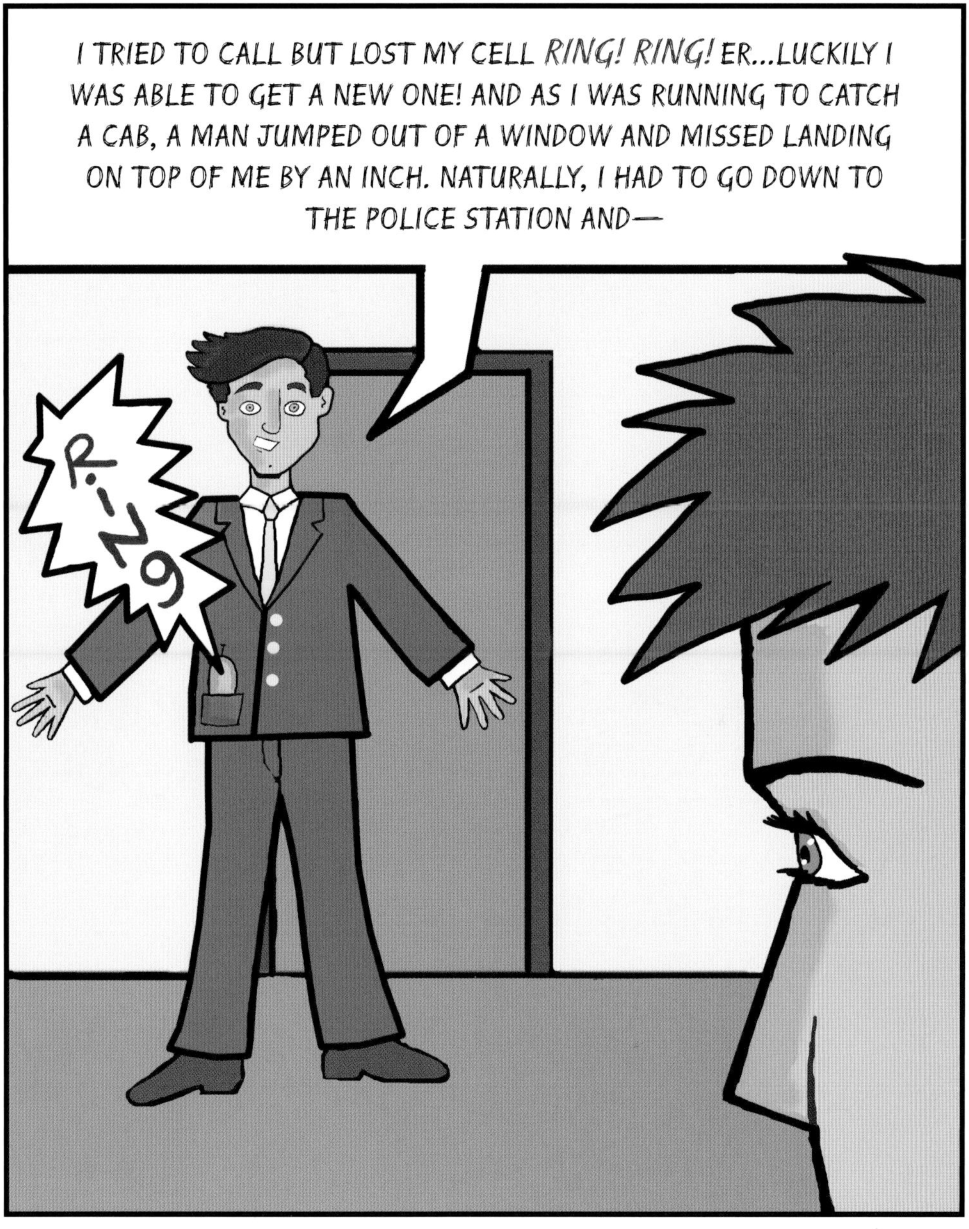

I wish I could say I missed John, but that wouldn't be true. *I don't miss him at all.* In fact, if I weren't so depressed, I'd be dancing on the ceiling...

But I have too many questions...

Why didn't I know he was cheating? How could I have been so stupid? Why did I marry John in the first place?

I know it's a cliché to always blame "the mother" but in my case she deserves a huge chunk...

The only "lullaby" she ever sang was...

On the first day of school my head was spinning with her words of wisdom...

In high school she knew what was important...

When I graduated from college husbandless...

I wanted to make my mother happy so I brought home a bevy of boyfriends for her approval. She gave them "the drill."

BOYFRIEND #1

BOYFRIEND #2

BOYFRIEND #3

My mother was a harsh critic.

None of them made the grade.

Finally, I brought home a live one. She gave John "the drill."

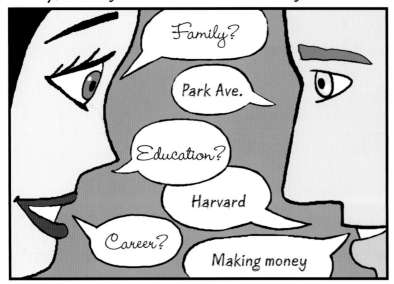

John passed with flying colors! *My mother could barely believe her good fortune.* My job was to reel "this one" in.

My mother became my full-time coach. All I had to do was follow her simple rules.

1. Do not accept a date later than Wednesday for Saturday night.
2. Never say "I love you" first.
3. Be unavailable.

I followed her rules to the letter. When John called on Thursday, one day late...

I waited till he said...

And I was unavailable...

My mother's rules worked! John fell for me hook, line, and sinker.

Did I get married to make my mother happy?... to make her proud? ...to finally shut her up?

My name is Jo Hudson. This is my first full-blown, over-the-top, wallow in self-pity depression. I have been in bed for three days except to go to the bathroom and kitchen, which *thank God!* are not far from my bed.

I am a freelance photographer. One good thing about being freelance is you can stay in bed all day and no one would notice. One bad thing is you can stay in bed all day and no one would notice.

Ironically, I've become the "it" bridal photographer.
Brides everywhere are desperate for me to photograph them.

And yes, that really is John's Rocket Scientist. That is one
wedding I can forego, although shooting Candy is tempting.

I only shoot black and white.

Everybody tells me I'm an "artist"...

...but *Picasso* is an artist.

There are two "must" shots when photographing the bride. The first is the Beauty Shot. She must look beautiful, radiant, and confident.

This is the photograph that lasts for Eternity. It goes on the mantel above the fireplace. It is the photograph that is passed from generation to generation so that one day little Lucy or Lance will say, "Grandma, you were a Beautiful Bride."

The second "must" shot is the bride and groom. This one can be either playful or serious as long as they connect through the eyes.

This photograph speaks of their bond, their commitment for eternal bliss. It is the one that says, "Happily ever after."

I love sad photographs but most people like happy ones, especially at weddings.

Nobody wants a picture of a sad bride.

Happy Barbie Bride Lamp sat perched on my nightstand. She was the first thing I saw every morning and the last thing every night.

I memorized every detail of the dress. The bride wore a white satin gown that fell gracefully on her tiny hips. Her neckline was V-shaped with 12 perfect buttons running down the back. She held a corsage of white roses to match the white roses that graced her veil.

We had so much in common, Barbie Bride Lamp and me. We both loved boys named Kenny...

...we both loved animals, real and stuffed...

...and we both were pure in body and soul.

I wasn't exactly sure what a virgin was but had a pretty good idea of what you were if you weren't one.

Also, if it was good enough for the Virgin Mary, then it was good enough for Barbie Bride Lamp and me.

It was shocking when years later I heard the news! It was the lead story...

Why did Barbie Bride Lamp betray me? Why didn't she marry Ken? Did she know all along she would be making a big mistake? Is a lamp smarter than me?

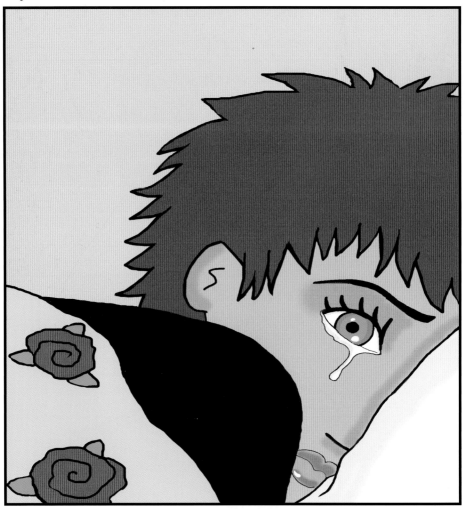

The first time I went into therapy was because all my friends were doing it.

Name: Andrea Hopkins
Job: Plus-size model
Age: 29
Marital Status: Single
Height: 5'10"
Weight: 185
Life Goal: For every woman to accept her own body

Name: Timothy Miller
Job: Homemaker and dad
Age: 33
Marital Status: Married (Gay)
Life Goal: To raise his child to be happy and well-adjusted

Name: Georgia D'Bella
Job: Zookeeper
Age: 30
Marital Status: Single
Life Goal: For humans to be kind to animals

Doctor Rubenstein diagnosed me.

I was so grateful. I couldn't wait to tell my friends!

First I told Andrea...

then Tim...

and finally Georgia...

I was happy with my self-esteem issue, but secretly wasn't sure what self-esteem meant.

After a few more sessions, I quit therapy. Not only was it expensive but Andrea had moved on to AA. I followed in Al-Anon.

Do I do everything my friends do? Am I the world's biggest follower? Could I be world leader of all the followers?

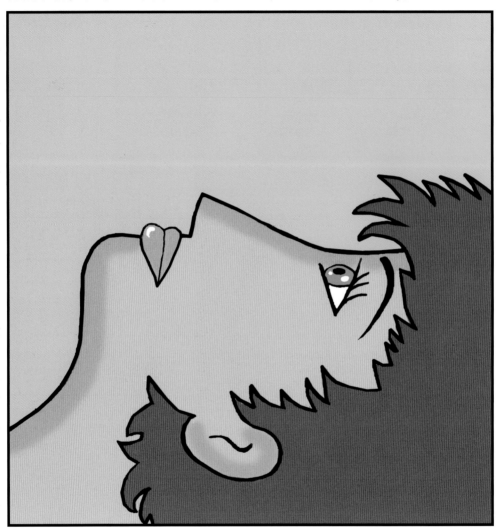

When my best friend Andrea got a dog, I wanted one too but my mother didn't. I bonded with Shorty while Andrea bonded with comic books.

I tried to hold on but...

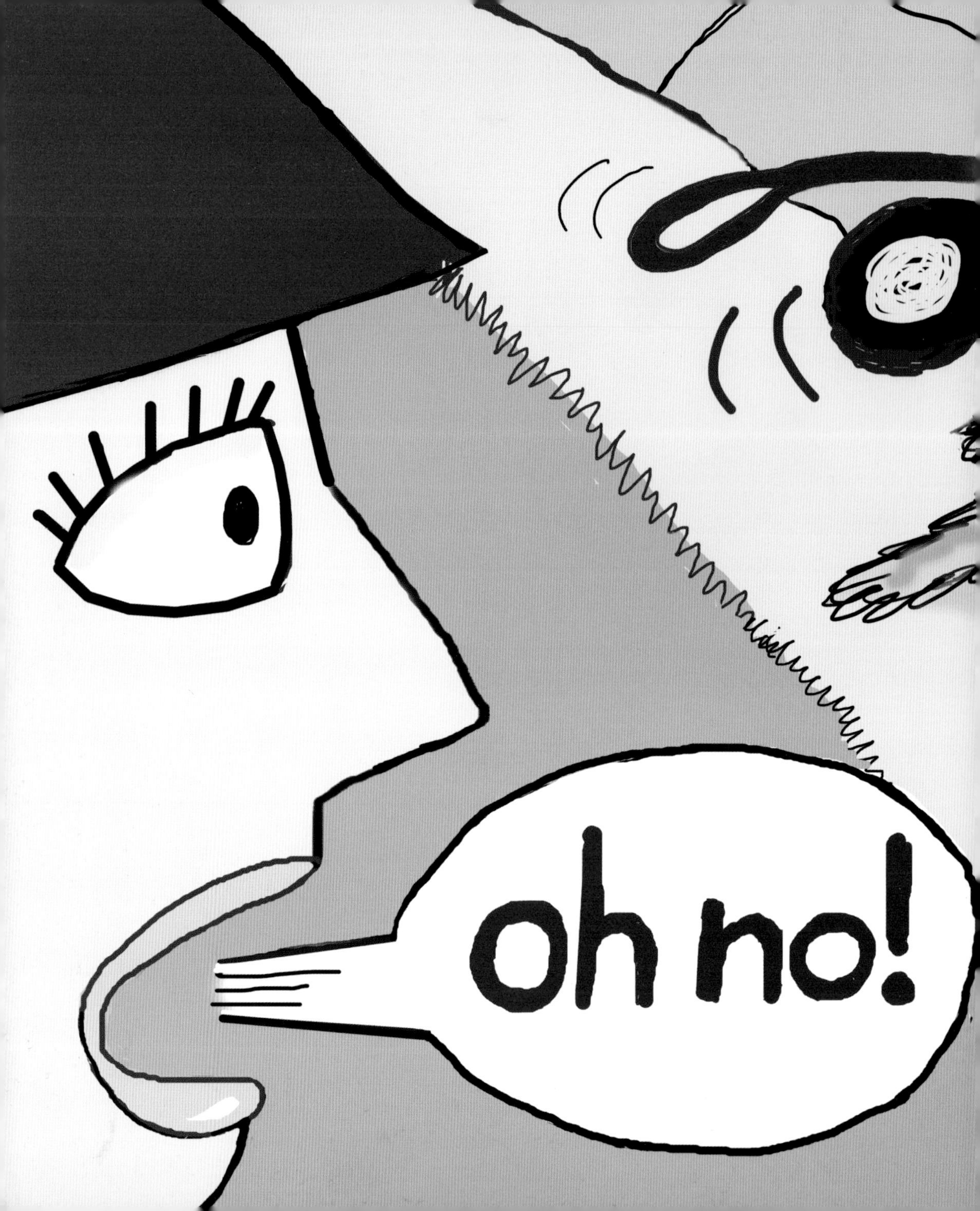
oh no!

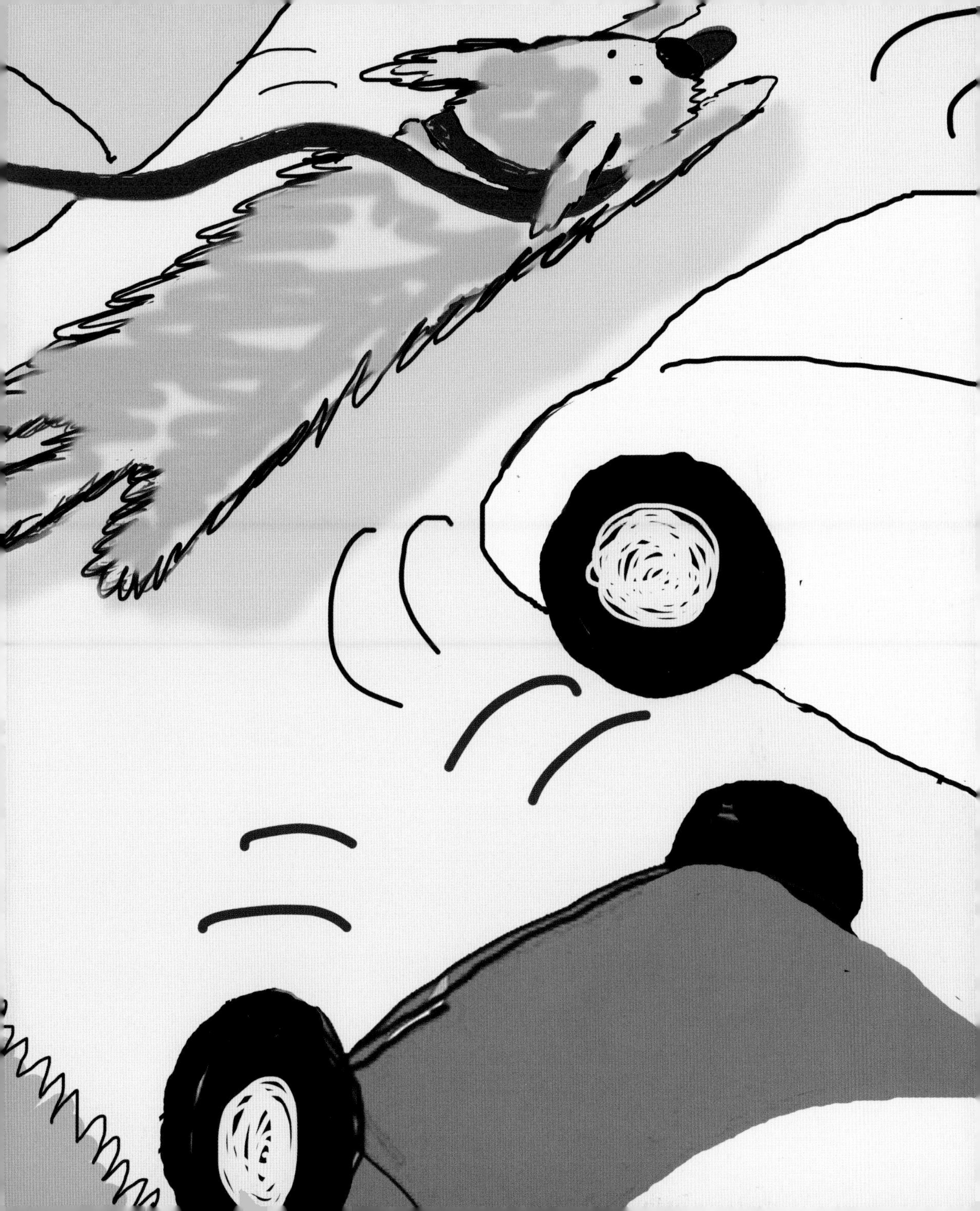

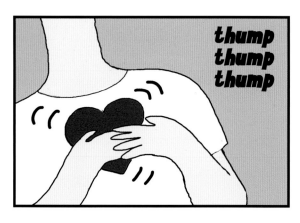

The world was slow now. Every pulsing second felt like an hour. *Shorty was going to get killed and it was all my fault.*

I couldn't look but had to! I saw cars zooming by but there was no sign of dead Shorty.

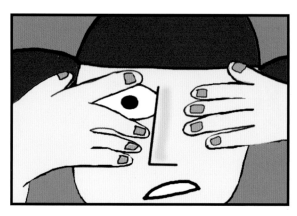

Across the street, *lo and behold*, there was Shorty. I couldn't believe my eyes! Shorty was alive! Alive I tell you!

I raced in between honking cars and screeching brakes. If Shorty could do this, so could I!

I wanted to hold Shorty. I wanted to hug Shorty. I wanted to tell Shorty to never do that again. But Shorty had found a friend.

I tried to separate them but they were huffing and puffing and couldn't be torn apart. It looked weird and creepy.

HELP!!!!!

Somehow Andrea's dad appeared from out of nowhere. He comforted me.

IT'S NOT YOUR FAULT. THE DOG WAS "IN HEAT."

ASK YOUR MOTHER.

I had no idea what "in heat" meant but I knew it had something to do with S-E-X.

My mother always spelled S-E-X whenever she talked about S-E-X. She handed me a book.

Read this. If you have any other questions, ask your father.

The Birds and Bees

I read all about the birds and bees but couldn't figure out what that had to do with Shorty.

I had questions so I took my mother's advice and asked my father.

There was only one thing left to do—ask Marjorie Katz. M. K. knew everything about everything. The only problem asking M. K. anything was that she would know I knew nothing about everything. But I swallowed my pride and asked anyway.

It was disgusting! It was gross! I hated Marjorie Katz. She *had* to be wrong.

Why is Shorty forever implanted in my brain? Is it possible to ever forget the "Shorty story"? Is it a dog-eat-dog world afterall?

My friends worried about me. Apparently, spending most of my waking hours in bed was a sure sign of depression. They had the answer.

First Andrea...

then Tim...

...and finally Georgia.

I'd never had a *Slam! Bam! Thank you, Man.* The thought of doing it with a total stranger seemed vacuous, empty, and dangerous. And yet, all my friends had done it at least once and lived to tell the tale. In fact, they loved telling the tale.

If getting laid could cure my depression, I was ready to give it a whirl.

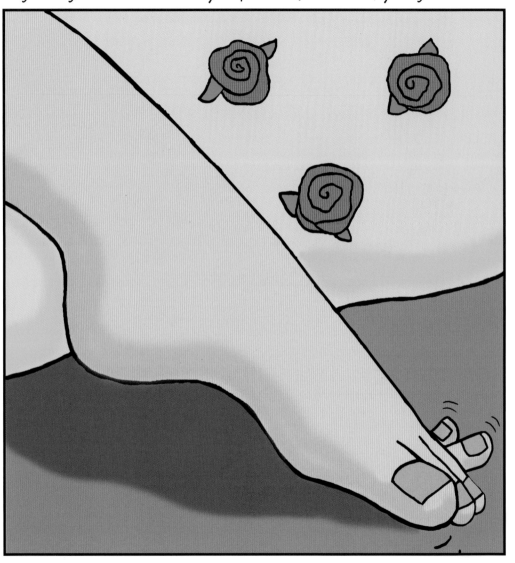

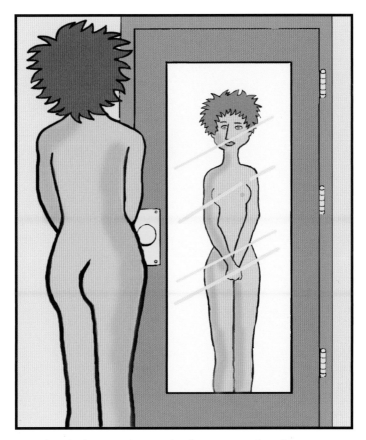

My body looked good. Apparently, depression made me lose weight. Had I known that, this would not have been my first.

I was jogging for about 5 minutes when I felt his eyes scanning my body. I smiled and he jogged beside me. He was cute, *really* cute. Then he said those four magical words...

We ran together for about one-sixteenth of a mile and then went back to my apartment. It was heaven! He came three times, I came twice. I couldn't wait till he left.

Immediately I called my friends with the great news. They were so proud of me. My friends were right! Getting laid *was* all I needed!

Life was grand until...

I reminded him about his girlfriend. He said she didn't need to know. I explained that he was a one-afternoon thing. He sent flowers. Finally, when he camped out at my door, I threatened to track down his girlfriend and deliver my very own "message from hell."

Yes, I had sunk as low as Candy. I was too embarrassed to tell my friends that I had failed miserably.

Getting laid is definitely not the answer.

We were 10. It was summertime. I climbed on the back of Kenny's bicycle and off we would go!

We stopped behind the garage, and there he kissed me gently on the cheek.

I thought I was going to faint from sheer ecstasy.

But I didn't want Kenny to think I was one of those fast slutty girls so I played it real cool.

When school began, Kenny started hanging around Linda. It hurt really bad.

I wanted to beg Kenny for just one more ride on his bicycle.

I wanted to pull out Linda's perfectly perfect ponytail.

But I did nothing except cry myself to sleep...

...dreaming only of Kenny.

Why didn't I kiss Kenny back? Was I too cool? Was Kenny the first of a long line of men who would betray me?

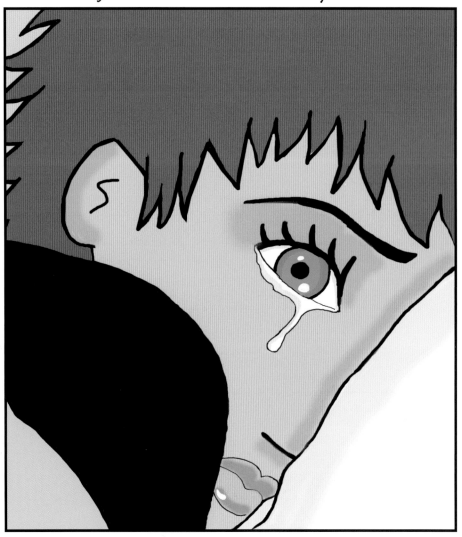

My photographs comfort me.

I have found other sad brides.

I'm happy I wasn't the only unhappy one.

Who were these brides?... What were they thinking?...
Were they in love?

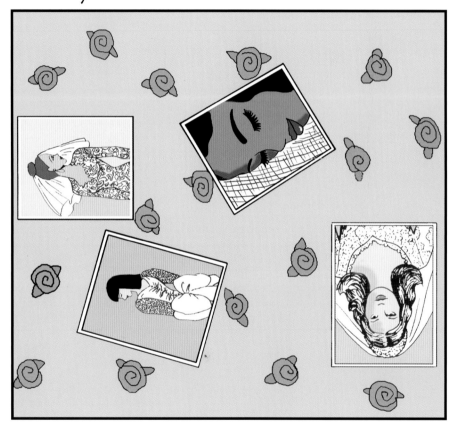

...or did they know all along that they were making a big mistake?

One day I asked, "Why are you sad?"

And she answered.

Because I'm still in love with Peter.

Then more sad brides chimed in...

...and even more!

I am talking to photographs, and what is worse, they are talking back to me. Am I going insane?

In high school, Stanley was captain of the football team. Stanley wanted to score with my body. But they were *my* private parts... pure and sweet and pink. Nobody could touch them... *not even Stanley.*

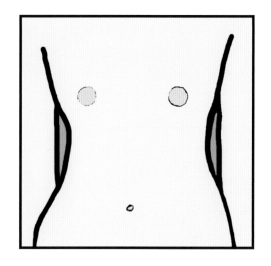

Thank God kissing was allowed because I loved kissing Stanley. He taught me how to use my tongue. I got really good at it. We once had a three-hour and twenty-minute make-out session!

Stanley wanted more. He told me his penis was turning blue. So I let Stanley feel my top private parts, *but only over my sweater.*

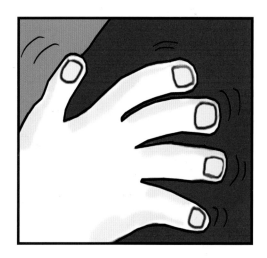

The morning after one of our record-breaking make-out sessions, I was walking to school with my best friend, Andrea.

Andrea tended to be overly dramatic so I was used to some believable "unbelievable" things.

I had to admit, that *was* unbelievable!

I felt sorry for Stephanie.

I felt superior to Stephanie.

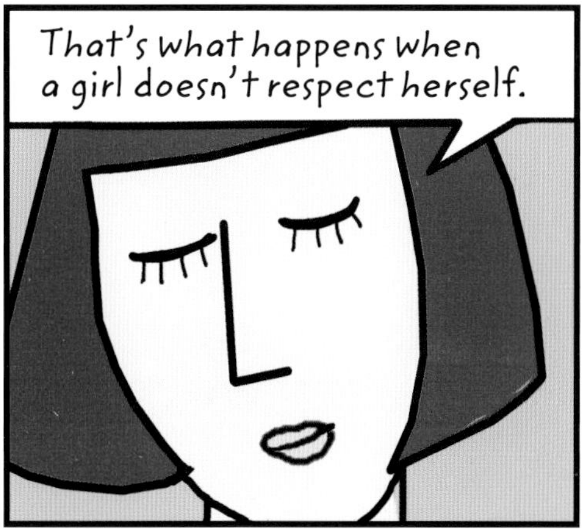
That's what happens when a girl doesn't respect herself.

I felt angry and slightly jealous.

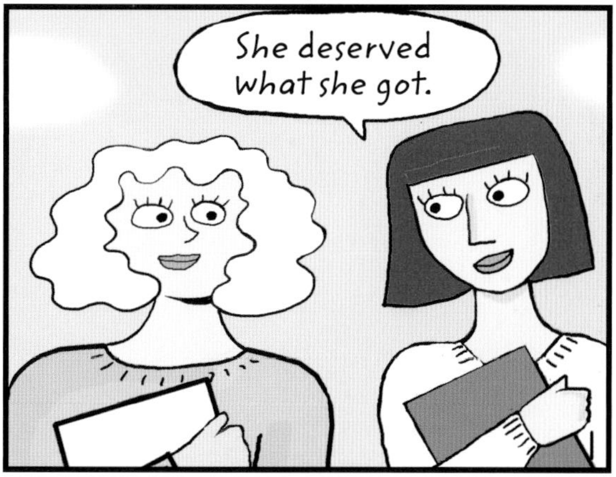
She deserved what she got.

Later that night, Stanley and I were well on our way to breaking our world-record-make-out session when Stanley came up for air.

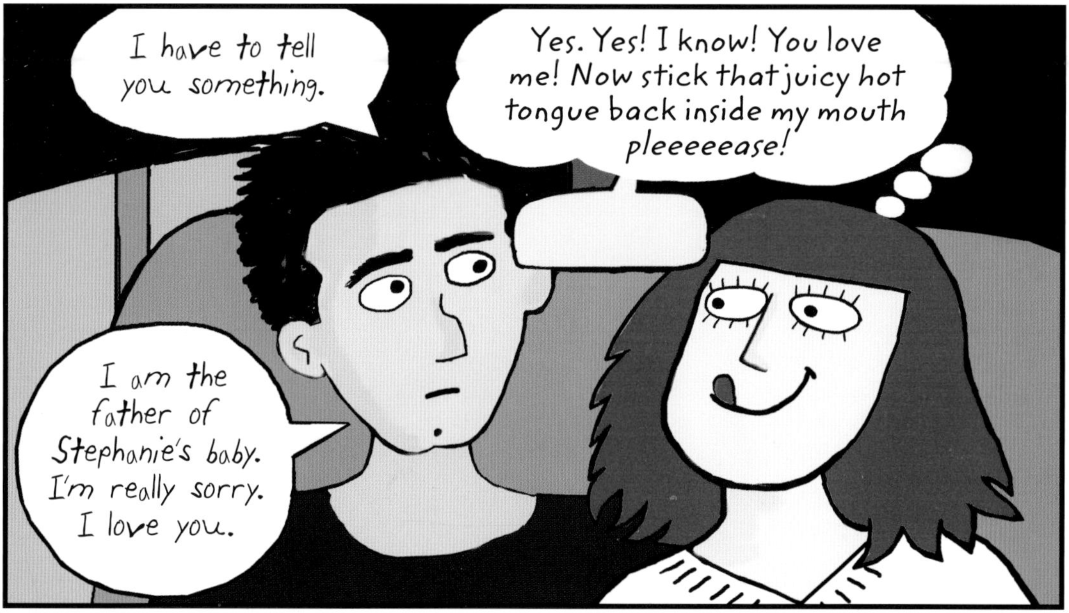
I have to tell you something.
Yes. Yes! I know! You love me! Now stick that juicy hot tongue back inside my mouth pleeeeease!
I am the father of Stephanie's baby. I'm really sorry. I love you.

I couldn't speak because my head started to swirl.

My body lifted and
I was floating above
the car. I could
see somebody who
appeared to be me
but it couldn't be me.

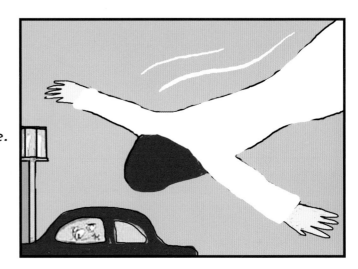

Her heart was bleeding so heavy, she *had* to be dead.

The next morning, I wasn't going to let anybody think I was upset that Stanley had gotten the slut pregnant.

I had an image to uphold! I couldn't show my true feelings, *not even to my best friend*. I knew if I ever showed them, then I could never take them back. I would be fully exposed... my naked self... out there for the universe to gobble up.

So I moved on to Lance. Lance was sweet. Lance was cute. Lance was a lousy kisser. But I taught him well and soon we were kissing just like Stanley and I used to... *well, almost.*

I wanted Stanley to see me with Lance. I wanted him to see how happy we were, Lance and me.

I wanted Stanley's heart to bleed the way my heart bled for him.

Finally, it was prom. Lance and I were dancing when I saw them walk in, Stanley and Stephanie. She was so big, I thought she'd pop the baby right there on the floor.

I didn't want to look at him, but I couldn't help myself. From across the room, our eyes locked.

At that moment, we both knew that we had lost our dream, each other, our once-in-a-lifetime. I booked a room for Lance and me. *It should have been Stanley.*

Lance stuck his penis into my vagina, where he bounced up and down for about 3 seconds until he exploded with white slime. *Marjorie Katz was right after all.*

Would "it" have been beautiful with Stanley? Why wasn't *he* my first? What was I saving it for? Do good girls finish last?

When I finally admitted to my friends that I had failed miserably with my "Slam! Bam! Thank you, Man" they were really worried. I didn't have the heart to mention the babbling brides. It was time to get back on the couch.

First it was Andrea (who dropped AA and was back in therapy)...   then Tim...

You can see Doctor Malamur. He has a waiting list till 2022 but I got you in for tomorrow at 8 o'clock.

You'll love Joy! She treats all the stars! Even Liza!

and finally Georgia...

Her name is Doctor Judy.

I decided to interview all three therapists. I'd ask the same question and the one who answered correctly got the grand prize of me for a patient. I wasn't sure what the answer was but felt fairly confident that once I heard it, I'd know.

Therapist #1: Doctor Malamar

Unfortunately, I couldn't tell the forest from the husband. Dr. Malamar was not for me.

Therapist #2: Joy

It was the way she said YOU that made me want to come up with a good answer.

I barely had time to think when Joy interjected...

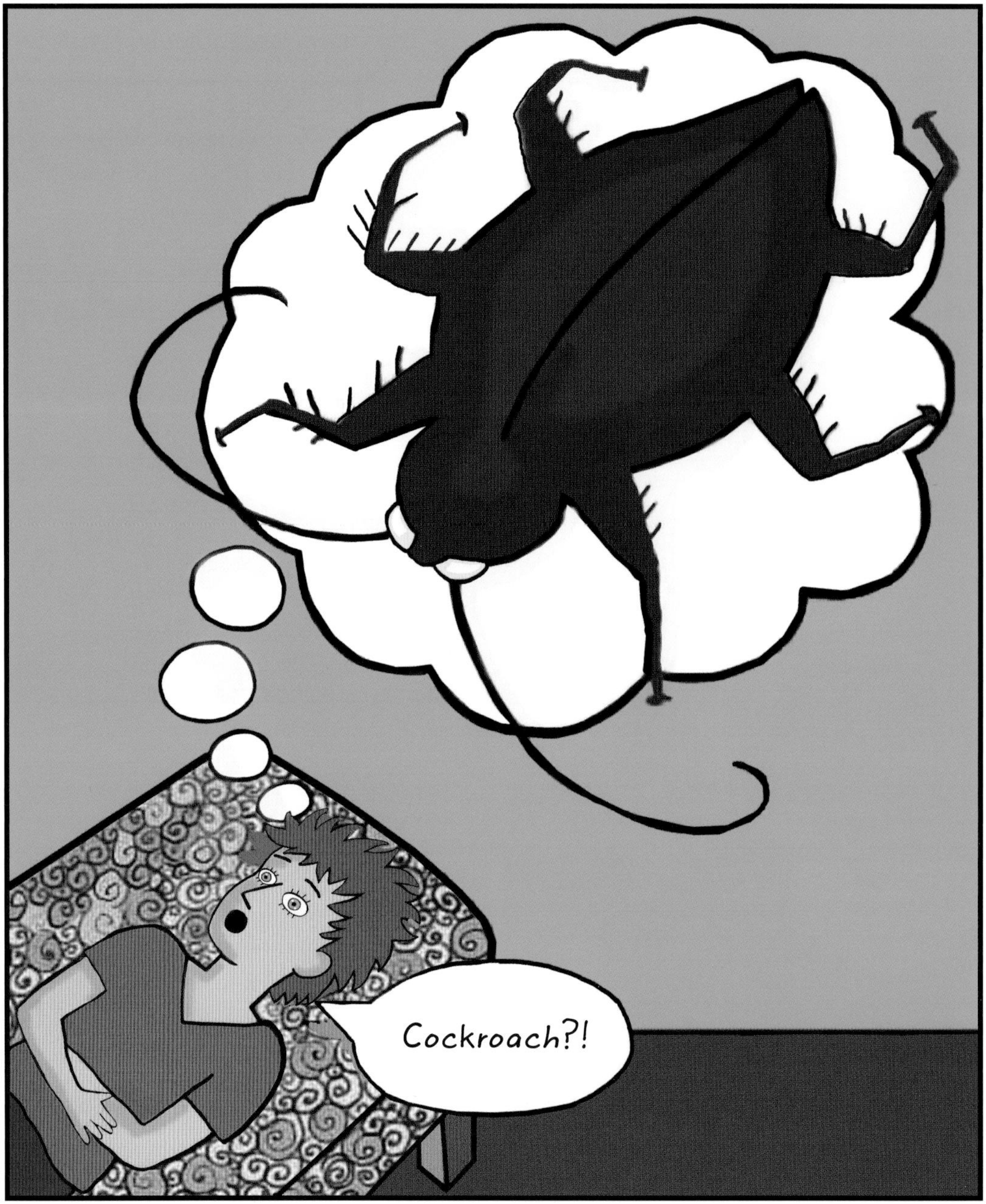
Cockroach?!

John would eye that sucker and...

...that roach was history.

I knew I was depressed, but I didn't think antidepressant depressed.
I was not happy with Joy.

Therapist #3: Doctor Judy

I didn't even have to ask the question when...

Doctor Judy listened.

Doctor Judy understood.

Doctor Judy sympathized.

And the winner, hands down, Dr. Judy.

She suggested 3 times a week.

Senior year, the popular crowd didn't get why I walked with weird William. After all, I was a *cheerleader!* I had an image to uphold.

But William's mom was Inez.

Inez was an artist. She was wild and wonderful. Her name used to be Ida till she changed it.

Inez's house was disheveled. She didn't care.
Her pipes were always breaking down.

I didn't understand Inez's poetry but it made
me cry.

Aside from being a cheerleader, I was also my high school yearbook photographer.

I was never without my camera. I shot people... that's Linda and Kenny! Still together after all these years.

...places...

...and things.

Inez studied my photographs.

When she said...

I *almost* believed her.

When I was with Inez, I *almost* felt like an artist.

One day when William and I went to his
house, it was empty.

Then he handed me a note.

William and I bonded. We both missed Inez terribly.

William also changed his name… to Willow, after his sex change.

Willow was one of my eight bridesmaids at my wedding.

I turned to my mother for sympathy.

Was being an artist out of the picture? Was I destined to be a cheerleader? Is it possible to be a cheerleader and an artist?

This time on the couch, I loved therapy! I could rag on my mother for 45 minutes straight and Doctor Judy listened. She was a captive audience.

Week 1

Week 2

Week 3

But after Week 3, I could see that even Doctor Judy was growing bored of my endless tirades against my mother.

Doctor Judy asked... Luckily, I had the answer...

I hadn't but I figured it was worth a shot.

Doctor Judy persisted.

The questions were getting harder. I wanted to give Doctor Judy the right answer but I was stumped.

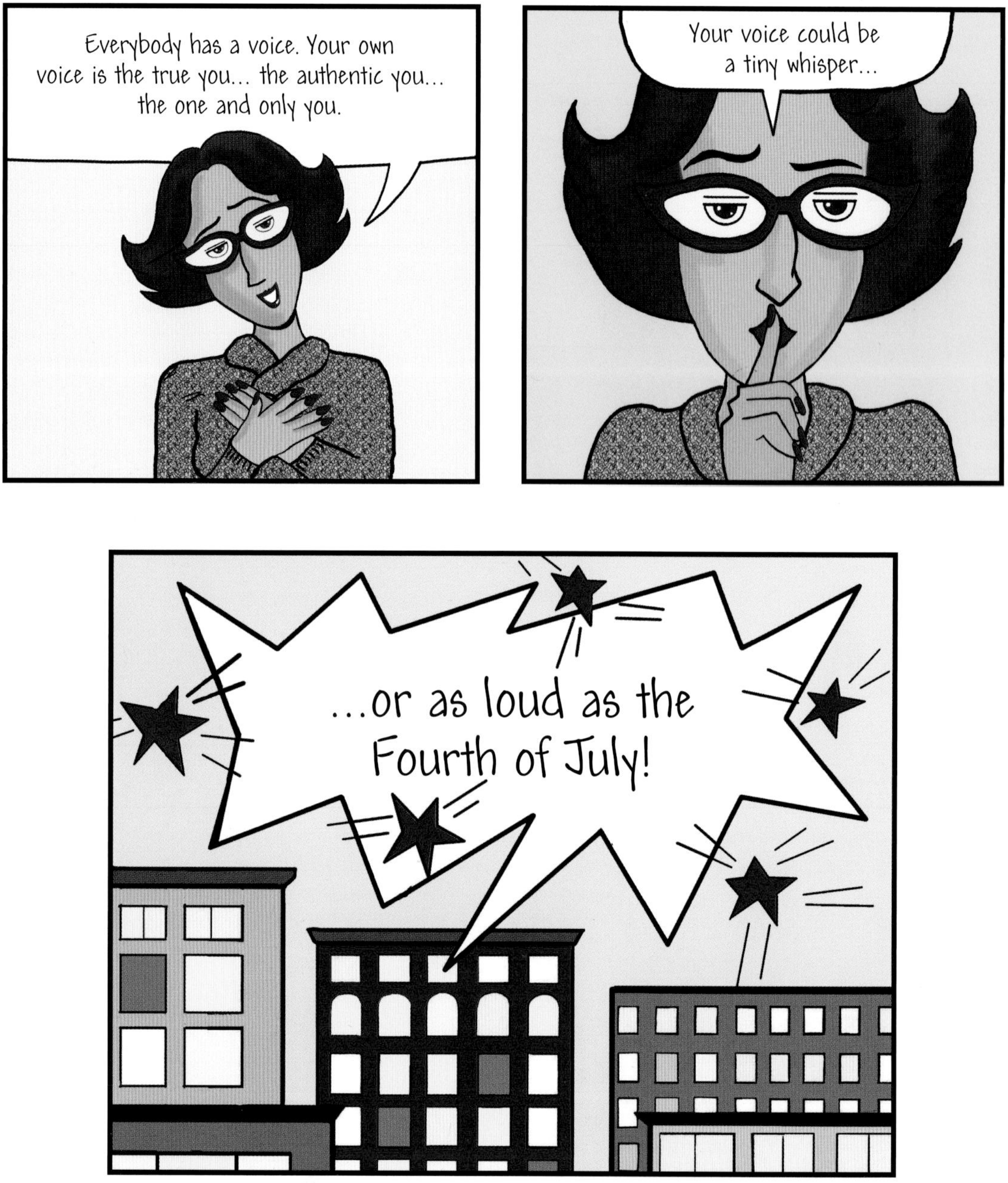
Everybody has a voice. Your own voice is the true you... the authentic you... the one and only you.
Your voice could be a tiny whisper...
...or as loud as the Fourth of July!

Doctor Judy was beginning to get on my nerves. Just because she hears voices, doesn't mean everybody on the planet hears them.

I bought the spray.

Back at the box, I turned my key and...

Right on cue, a mammoth roach darted across the floor as if to taunt me, as if to remind me who had the power.

Suddenly, I felt a calm come over me... I live here.

I did not scream... This is my box.

I did not run to my bed and wrap myself around my sheets and count to 100... I am not chicken.

I grabbed my weapon of mass destruction and...

It was a direct hit. I killed him dead.

Now, what do I do with the body?

I decided to leave it where it lay, to warn cockroaches all over my box that there was a new sheriff in town.

When I moved to the city, the whole world opened up to me.

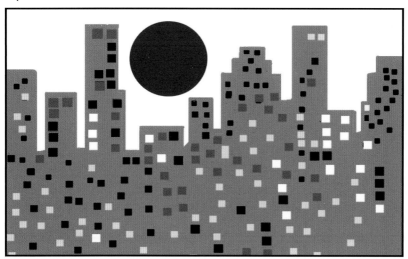

I worked in a photo lab where I got to handle and look at great photographs. My favorites were by the world-renowned photographer Pablo. He was a genius with shadow and light.

Pablo's photographs were so beautiful, I cried.
Carefully, though, so that my tears wouldn't fall over the art.

Pablo's photographs made me feel like I was present in the picture...

And Pablo's photographs were planted indelibly in my brain so I could see them forever.

One day Pablo *himself* walked into the photo lab. My knees were shaking so hard, I thought I would pass out right there on the spot!

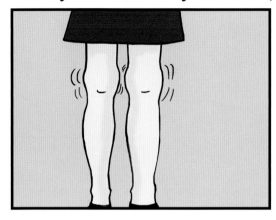

I didn't think I could possibly utter a word but somehow managed.

Granted they were stupid words but Pablo seemed to like them.

After work I stopped by. He told me to sit. It was surreal. Pablo *himself* was shooting me!

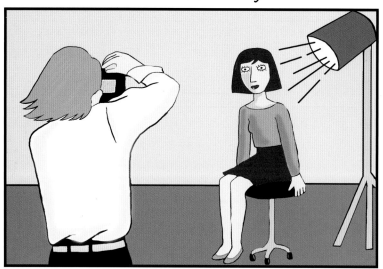

Pablo instructed me about light...

Pablo showed me shadow...

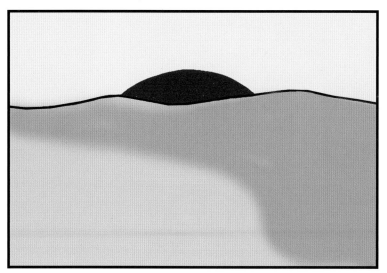

And Pablo taught me how to make love... *real love.*

He was 55 and I was 25. I was hooked.

My friends had their doubts. First Andrea...

...but he's really old.

I don't have a problem with our age difference. He's so youthful and vibrant. Sometimes I feel like I'm 55 and he's 25.

then Tim...

What if you want to have kids?

He already has two, but I'm sure he would have more for me.

and finally Georgia...

It's like a light inside me died, but with Pablo I am burning—

Suddenly, something caught my eye...

It was a man who *looked* like Pablo...
but it must be a mistake. Pablo had a shoot.

It was a man who *dressed* like Pablo...
but it must be a mistake because he had his arm around a girl
who looked remarkably like Barbie.

It was a man who *walked* like Pablo... right by the window.
That was no mistake. It *was* Pablo.

*The girl was younger than me! Apparently Pablo didn't have a
problem with age difference either.*

Shooting helped me get over Pablo. I shot people...

...places...

...and things.

And at dusk, I watched the sun fall behind the buildings, to capture the light and shadow...

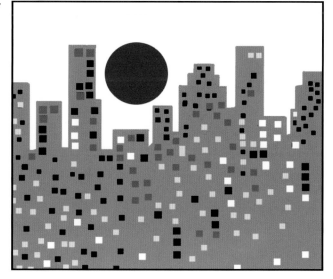

...and CLICK...

The moment was mine forever.

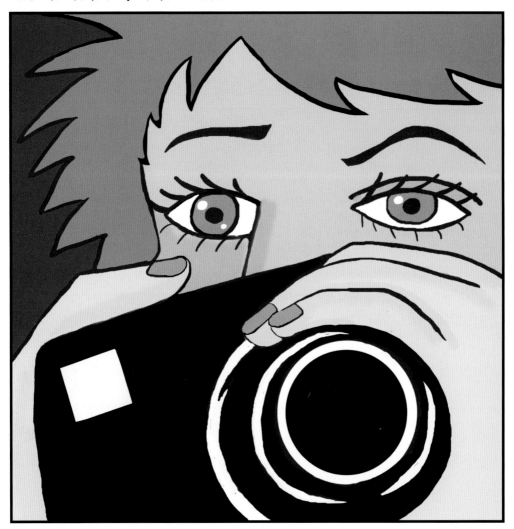

I was getting good at getting over a broken heart. Was that a good thing to be getting good at?

I was curious about Doctor Judy's so-called voices so I asked my friends.

Andrea had a voice...

I close my eyes, breathe deeply, and let in the light. Then my own voice softly speaks to me.

Tim had one too...

My own voice is right here. It's my gut. If I ignore my gut, I get into trouble.

And so did Georgia.

It's all basic instinct. Instinctively, birds fly, wolves howl at the moon, and mothers protect their young. If you call upon your instinct, instinctively it will come.

I wanted to find my own voice, but had no idea where to look so I decided to try out my friends' voices.

First, I tried Andrea's...

I closed my eyes, breathed deeply, and let in the light. But I heard nothing. My own voice didn't speak to me and neither did Andrea's for that matter.

Then Tim's...

I searched for my gut...

...but found my stomach instead.

Am I gutless?

And finally I gave a shout-out to Georgia's voice...

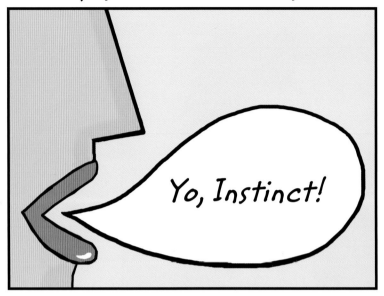

...but instinctively fell asleep.

All week long, I heard lots of voices...

...but none of them were mine.

Am I the only person on the planet without a Voice?

The sad brides were there to share my pain...

Bobby was my childhood sweetheart. We fell in love in first grade. We dated all through high school and college and planned our wedding the day after graduation. One night while he was on his way to pick me up, a drunk driver came out of nowhere and smashed my Bobby to death. I married his brother, George. I thought that maybe I could turn him into Bobby. But he was only George.

Another sad bride shared...

My parents thought I could do better so they kept pointing out his faults and pretty soon I was seeing what they were talking about. He really was a loser. But I didn't want to cancel the wedding because then my parents would be right.

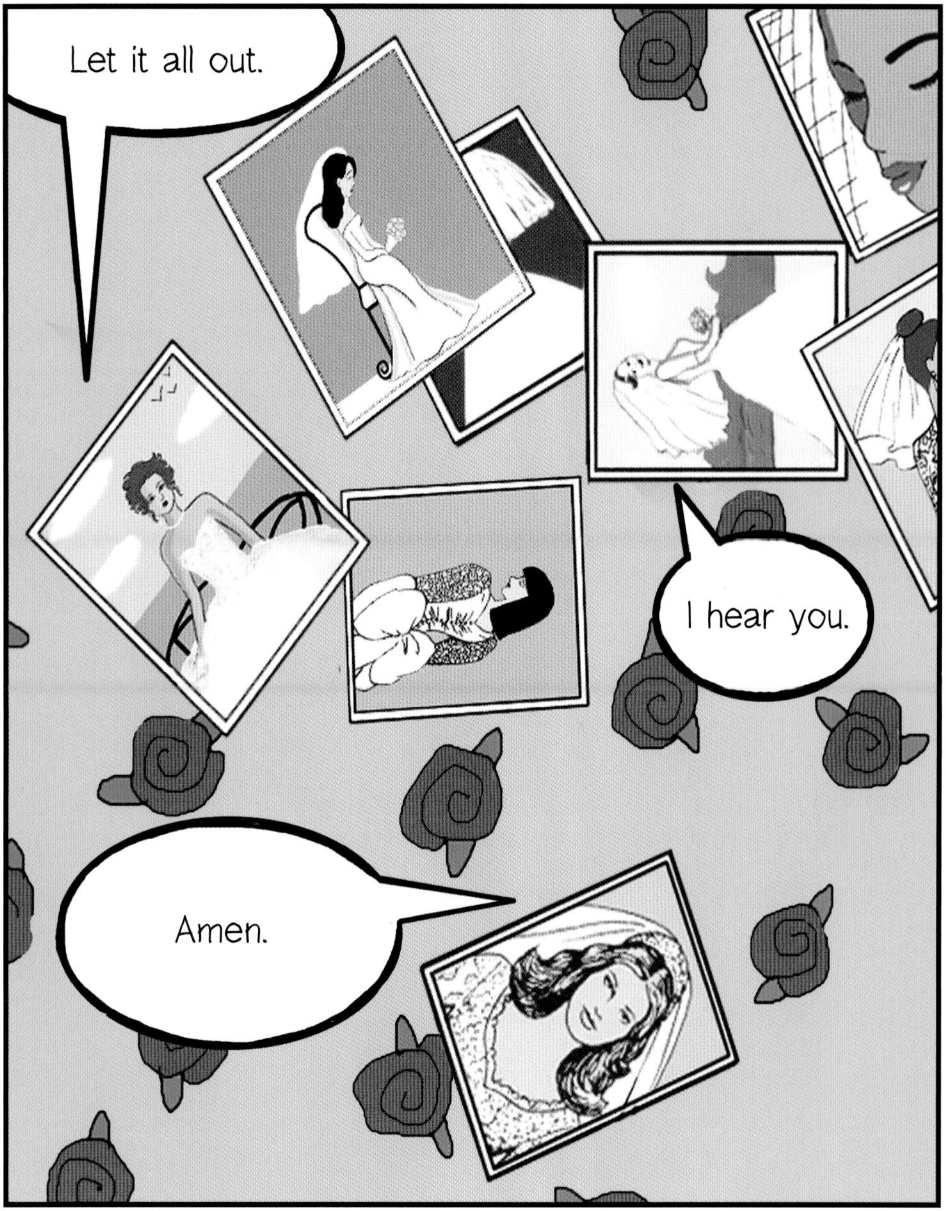
Let it all out.
I hear you.
Amen.

And then Molly shared...

We were secret soul mates for 8 beautiful years. I loved her from the bottom of my heart. But I couldn't admit I was a lesbian so I married him.

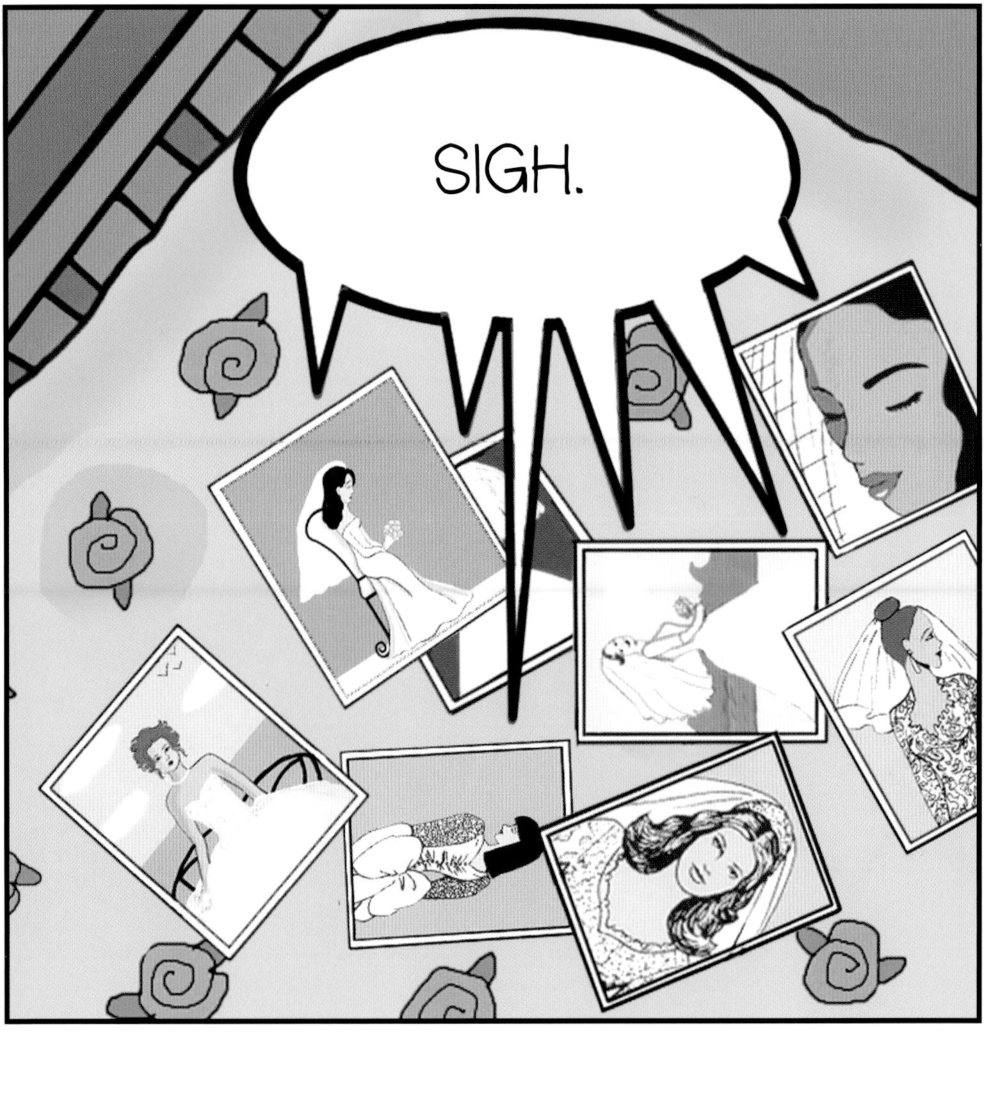
SIGH.

I was not ready to share.

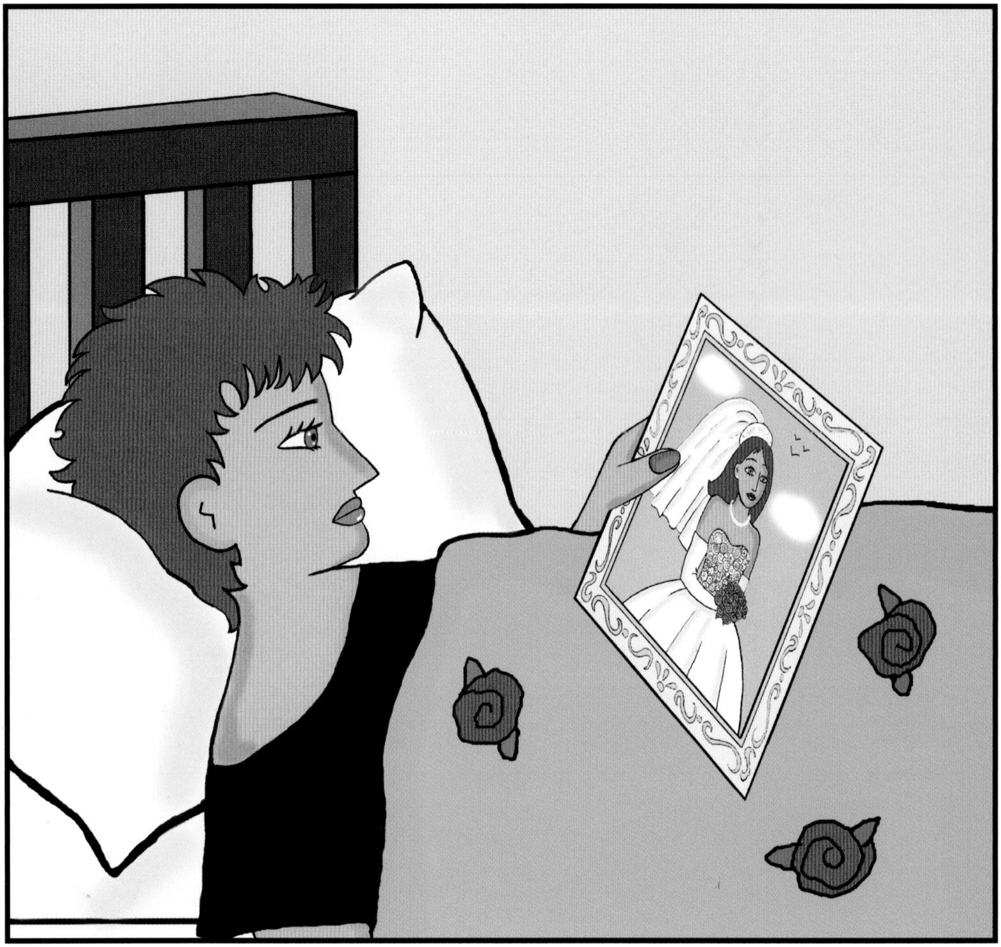

I knew it wasn't a good idea but I had nowhere to run, nowhere to hide. So my mother and I went shopping...

...and did lunch.

I tried to talk to my mother about my feelings.

I tried to talk to my mother about my work...

...but it was hopeless.

I was sinking...

sinking fast...

couldn't breathe...

drowning...

I had one last gasp and...

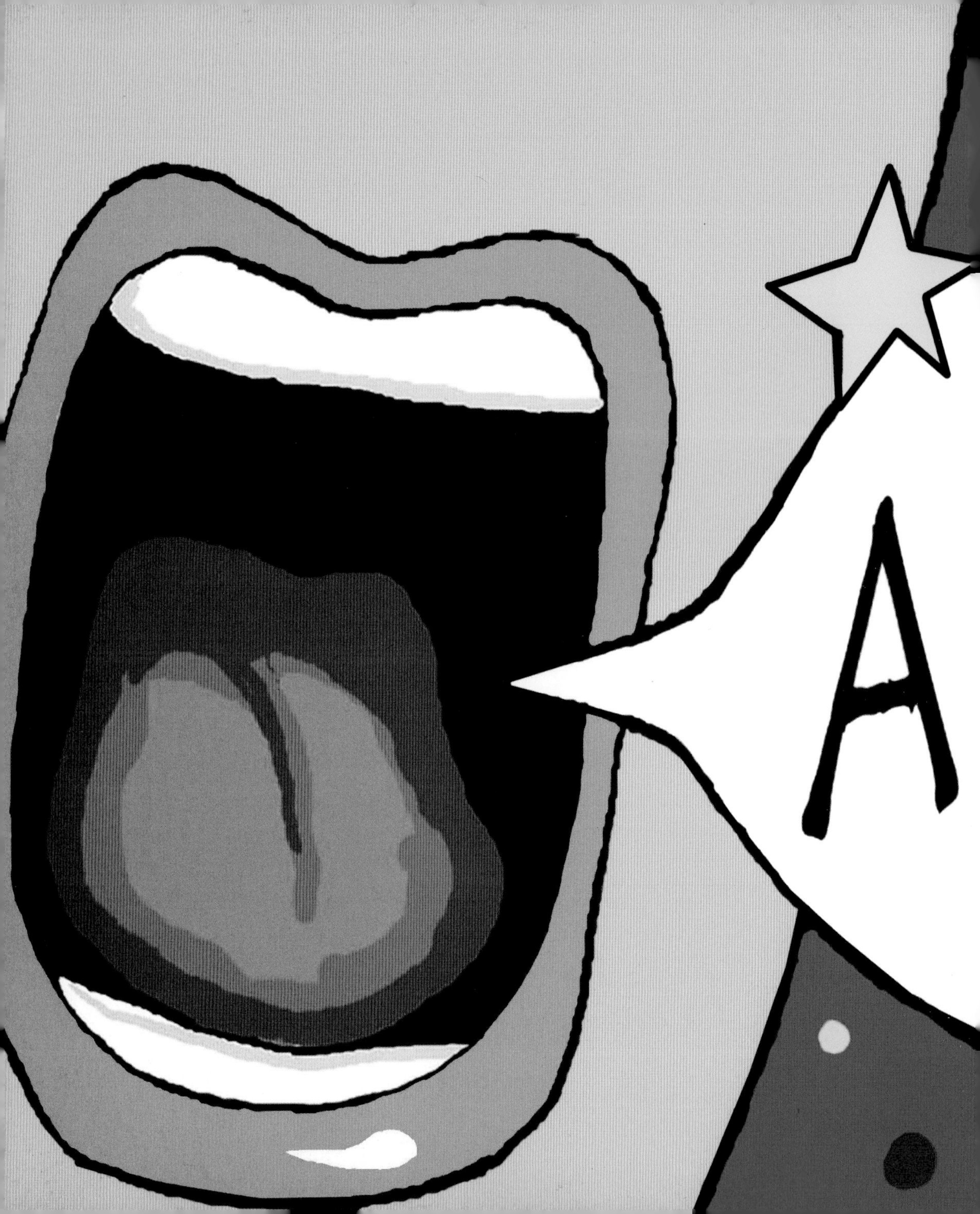
A

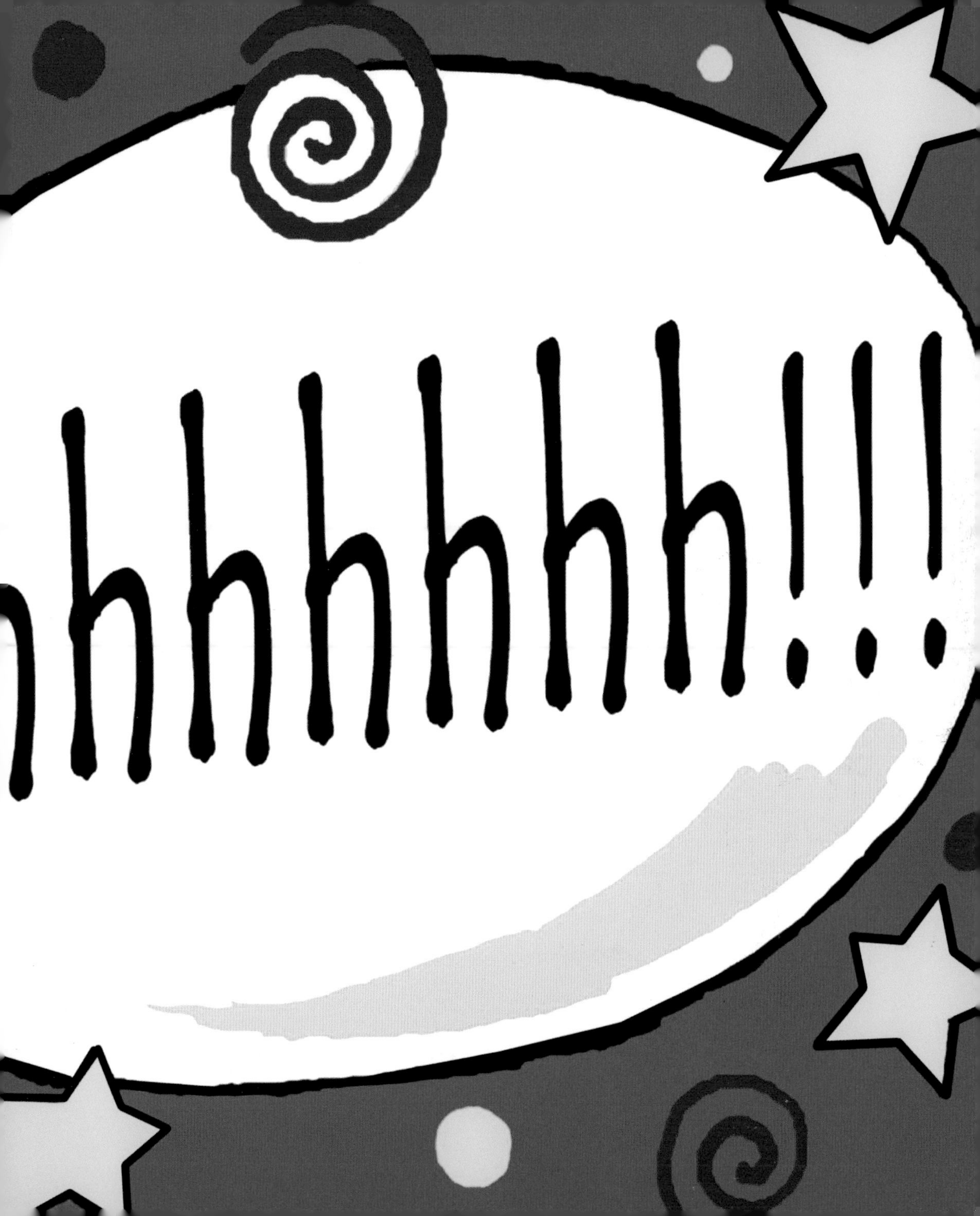
hhhhhhh!!!

I saw the look of horror on my mother's face...
but I couldn't stop screaming.
Everybody in the restaurant stopped eating...
but I couldn't stop screaming.
The maitre d' rushed us out (his treat!)...
but I couldn't stop screaming.

I sobbed all the way home.

My mother took care of me.

And then she left.

Am I totally out of control? Or was I screaming to get out?
Am I out? Or in-sane?

Suddenly, from out of the blue...

you listened to your
friends you listened
to the man on the
moon you listened
to the mother from
hell everyBody
except your
VERY OWN
Voice

I got tired of not being heard so checked out till your PRIMAL scream woke me from a dead sleep. This is it... your last chance Ready to listen?

Suddenly, it all came back to me like a crashing wave against my skull.

I remembered my own voice when it said...

When I won an art scholarship...

It was true. I listened to my mother.

And I remembered when John proposed, my own voice shouted...

It was even there when I said...

It was hard to admit the truth. I just wasn't listening.

I should have been dancing on the ceiling...

...yet my depression was the only thing that felt all mine.

My pillow feels safe and secure...

...my comforter comforts me...

...and the brides are my constant companions.

I would have preferred a kinder, softer voice, but since I'd been hoping, and searching, and longing for My Own Voice, when it shouted...

Exercise
see friends
show the
world your
art

...I decided to listen.

So I went jogging in Central Park.

I was ready to head for the hills when My Own Voice purred...

I couldn't believe my ears! But since I decided to listen, I asked...

We did.
It was heaven!

Then we went back to my place. He came two times, I came three. I didn't want him to leave.

I caught up with friends. First Andrea...

...then Tim...

...and finally Georgia.

It *was* good to see them.

And back in the box, My Own Voice appreciated my photographs...

And I confessed...

My Own Voice disagreed...

My Own Voice made a lot of sense.

And the brides added their two cents.

I was ready to show the world my art! So I
went to galleries on the East Side, West Side...

...uptown, downtown.

I went to galleries in Soho, Noho, Boho, and Ohno...

...Brooklyn, Queens, and Staten Island.

One day while I was gallery gazing...

I peeked in and saw Pablo *himself*...

I was ready to head for the hills when My Voice engulfed me...

Easy for My Own Voice to say. My Own Voice hadn't been
humiliated by Pablo the Pig. On the other hand,
I wanted Pablo to see what a mature woman I'd become...
I wanted Pablo to see a strong woman who didn't hold grudges...
I wanted Pablo to see a woman who knew the score...

I wanted Pablo to see me.

I could tell by the way his eyes glazed over that he didn't know *or care* who I was.

I wanted to scream...

...but then remembered My Own Voice...

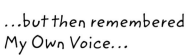

But then he saw the brides...

And Pablo murmured...

The brides and I answered in unison.

The next week...

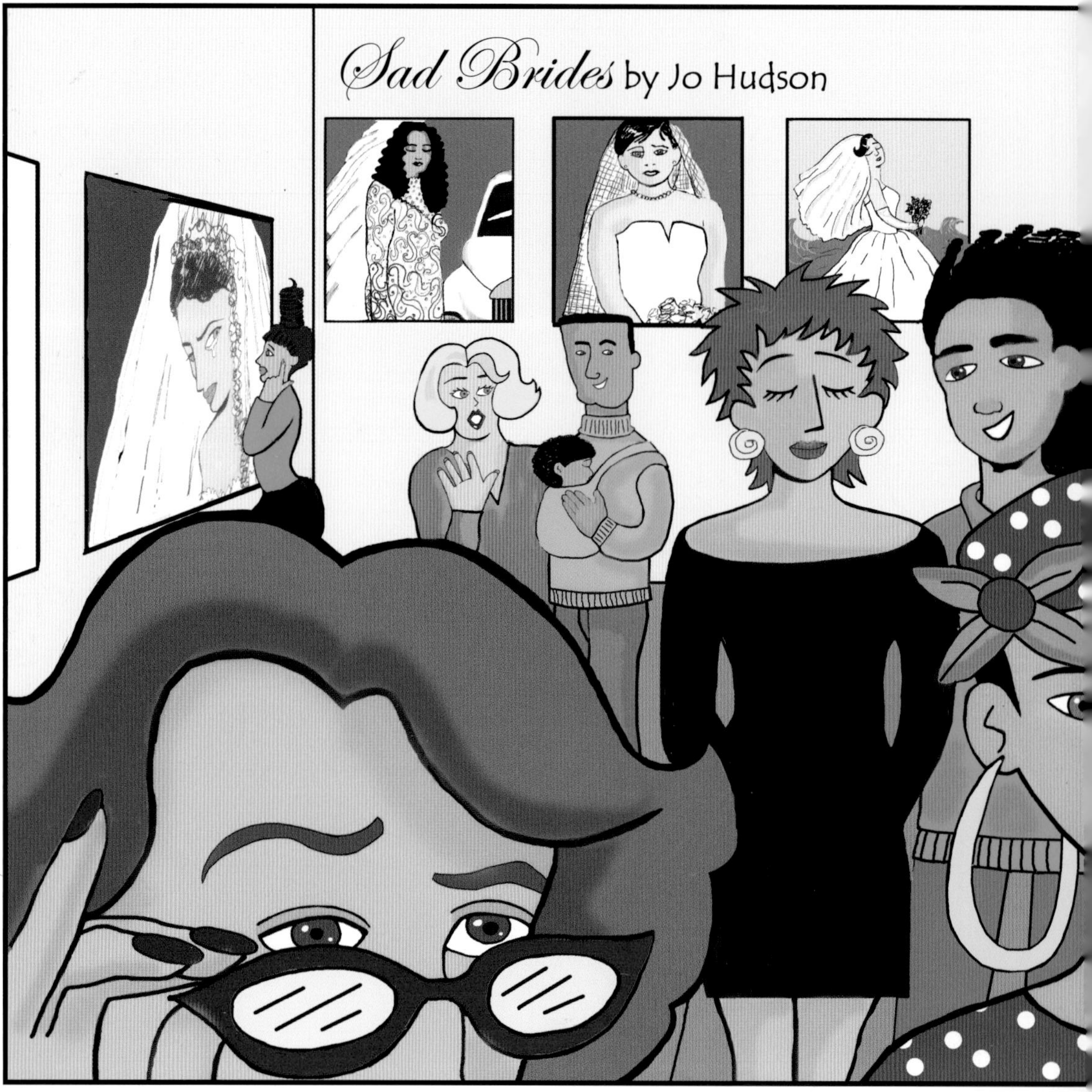
Sad Brides by Jo Hudson

My show was a huge success! Everybody who was there was there.

Later that night, I was finally ready to share...

I always wanted to be a bride, just like Barbie Bride Lamp. She wore a white satin gown that fell gracefully on her tiny hips. Her neckline was V-shaped with 12 perfect buttons running down the back. She held a corsage of white roses to match the white roses that graced her veil.

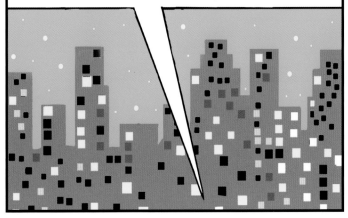

OMIGOD! Did I get married for the dress?

The End...